Prayer in the
Acts of the Apostles

by
Pope Benedict XVI

*All booklets are published thanks to the
generous support of the members of the
Catholic Truth Society*

CATHOLIC TRUTH SOCIETY
PUBLISHERS TO THE HOLY SEE

Contents

The Prayerful Presence of the Blessed Virgin 3

The Passover of the Lord 11

Little Pentecost. 19

The Primacy of Prayer and of the Word of God 26

The Testimony of St Stephen 34

The Imprisonment and Release of St Peter 40

All rights reserved. First published 2013 by The Incorporated Catholic Truth Society, 40-46 Harleyford Road London SE11 5AY Tel: 020 7640 0042 Fax: 020 7640 0046. © 2013 Libreria Editrice Vaticana. This edition © 2013 The Incorporated Catholic Truth Society.

ISBN 978 1 86082 863 8

The Prayerful Presence of the Blessed Virgin

Our Lady, Mother of all

In our continuing catechesis on Christian prayer, we now begin a new chapter on prayer in the *Acts of the Apostles* and later the *Letters of Saint Paul*. Today I wish to speak of the figure of Mary, who with the Apostles in the Upper Room prayerfully awaits the gift of the Holy Spirit. In all the events of her life, from the Annunciation through the cross to Pentecost, Mary is presented by St Luke as a woman of recollected prayer and meditation on the mystery of God's saving plan in Christ. In the Upper Room, we see Mary's privileged place in the Church, of which she is the "exemplar and outstanding model in faith and charity" (*Lumen Gentium*, 53). As Mother of God and Mother of the Church, Mary prays in and with the Church at every decisive moment of salvation history. Let us entrust to her every moment of our own lives, and let her teach us the need for prayer, so that in loving union with her Son we may implore the outpouring of the Holy Spirit and the spread of the Gospel to all the ends of the earth.

I would like to speak about prayer in the *Acts of the Apostles* and later in the *Letters of Saint Paul*. St Luke, as we know, has given us one of the four Gospels, dedicated to the earthly life of Jesus; but he has also left us what has been called the first book on the history of the Church; i.e., the *Acts of the Apostles*. In both of these books, one of the recurring elements is *prayer*, from that of Jesus to that of Mary, the disciples, the women and the Christian community.

Ascension

The beginning of the Church's journey is rhythmically marked by the action of the Holy Spirit, who transforms the Apostles into witnesses of the Risen One to the shedding of their blood, and also by the rapid spread of the word of God to the East and to the West. However, before the proclamation of the Gospel is spread abroad, Luke recounts the episode of the Ascension of the Risen One (cf. *Ac* 1:6-9). The Lord delivers to the disciples the programme of their lives, which are devoted to evangelisation. He says: "You shall receive power when the Holy Spirit has come upon you; and you shall be my witnesses in Jerusalem and in Judea and Samaria and to the end of the earth" (*Ac* 1:8). In Jerusalem, the Apostles, who were now eleven due to the betrayal of Judas Iscariot, were gathered together at home in prayer, and it is precisely in prayer that they await the gift promised by the Risen Christ, the Holy Spirit.

St Luke and the Virgin

Within this context of expectancy - between the Ascension and Pentecost - St Luke mentions *for the last time* Mary, the Mother of Jesus, and his brethren (v. 14). He had dedicated the beginning of his Gospel to Mary, from the announcement of the Angel to the birth and infancy of the Son of God made man. With Mary the earthly life of Jesus begins, and with Mary the Church's first steps are also taken; in both instances, the atmosphere is one of listening to God and of recollection. Today, therefore, I would like to consider this praying presence of the Virgin in the midst of the disciples who would become the first nascent Church.

The prayer of Mary

Mary quietly followed her son's entire journey during his public life, even to the foot of the cross; and now she continues in silent prayer to follow the Church's path. At the Annunciation in her home of Nazareth, Mary welcomes the angel of God; she is attentive to his words; she welcomes them and responds to the divine plan, thereby revealing her complete availability: "Behold, the handmaid of the Lord; let it be to me according to your word" (cf. *Lk* 1:38). Because of her inner attitude of listening, Mary is able to interpret her own history, and to humbly acknowledge that it is the Lord who is acting. In visiting her relative Elizabeth, she breaks forth into a prayer of praise and joy, and of celebration of the divine grace that filled her heart and her life, making her the Mother of the Lord (*Lk* 1:46-55). Praise, thanksgiving, joy: in the canticle of the *Magnificat*, Mary looks not only to what God has wrought in her, but also to what he has accomplished and continually accomplishes throughout history. In a famous commentary on the *Magnificat*, St Ambrose summons us to have the same spirit of prayer. He writes: "May the soul of Mary be in us to magnify the Lord; may the spirit of Mary be in us to exult in God" (*Expositio Evangelii secundum Lucam* 2, 26: PL 15, 1561).

Recollection and meditation

Also in the Cenacle in Jerusalem, in the "upper room where [the disciples of Jesus] were staying" (cf. *Ac* 1:13), in an atmosphere of listening and prayer, she is present, before the doors are thrown open and they begin to announce the Risen Lord to all peoples, teaching them to observe all that the Lord had commanded (*Mt* 28:19-20). The stages in Mary's journey - from the home of Nazareth to that in Jerusalem, through the cross where her son entrusts to her the Apostle John - are marked by her ability to maintain a persevering atmosphere of recollection, so that she might ponder each event in the silence of her heart before God (cf. *Lk* 2:19-51) and in meditation before God, also see the will of God therein and be able to accept it interiorly. The presence of the

Mother of God with the Eleven following the Ascension is not, then, a simple historical annotation regarding a thing of the past; rather, it assumes a meaning of great value, for she shares with them what is most precious: the living memory of Jesus, in prayer; and she shares this mission of Jesus: to preserve the memory of Jesus and thereby to preserve his presence.

Mary and the Holy Spirit

The final mention of Mary in the two writings of St Luke is made on the sabbath day: the day of God's rest after Creation, the day of silence after the Death of Jesus and of expectation of his resurrection. The tradition of remembering Holy Mary on Saturday is rooted in this event. Between the Ascension of the Risen One and the first Christian Pentecost, the Apostles and the Church gather together with Mary to await with her the gift of the Holy Spirit, without whom one cannot become a witness. She who already received him in order that she might give birth to the incarnate Word, shares with the whole Church in awaiting the same gift, so that "Christ may be formed" (*Ga* 4:19) in the heart of every believer. If the Church does not exist without Pentecost, neither does Pentecost exist without the Mother of Jesus, since she lived in a wholly unique way what the Church experiences each day under the action of the Holy Spirit. St Chromatius of Aquilea comments on the annotation found in the Acts of the Apostles in this way: "The Church was united in the upper room with Mary, the Mother of Jesus, and with his brethren. One, therefore, cannot speak of the Church unless Mary, the Mother of the Lord, is present ... The Church of Christ is there where the Incarnation of Christ from the Virgin is preached, and where the Apostles who are the brothers of the Lord preach, there one hears the Gospel" (*Sermon* 30, 1: SC 164, 135).

'A singular member of the Church'

The Second Vatican Council wished to emphasise in a particular way the bond that is visibly manifest in Mary and the Apostles praying together, in the same place, in expectation of the Holy Spirit. The Dogmatic Constitution *Lumen Gentium* affirms: "Since it has pleased God not to manifest solemnly the mystery of the salvation of the human race before he would pour forth the Spirit promised by Christ, we see the Apostles before the day of Pentecost 'persevering with one mind in prayer with the women and Mary the Mother of Jesus, and with his brethren' (*Ac* 1:14) and Mary by her prayers imploring the gift of the Spirit, who had already overshadowed her in the Annunciation" (n. 59). The privileged place of Mary is the Church, where "she is hailed as a pre-eminent and singular member of the Church, and as its type and excellent exemplar in faith and charity" (ibid, n. 53).

Mary can teach us to pray

Venerating the Mother of Jesus in the Church therefore means learning from her to become a community that prays: this is one of the essential marks in the first description of the Christian community as delineated in the *Acts of the Apostles* (cf. 2:42). Often, prayer is dictated by difficult situations, by personal problems that lead us to turn to the Lord for light, comfort and help. Mary invites us to expand the dimensions of prayer, to turn to God not only in times of need and not only for ourselves, but also in an undivided, persevering, faithful way, with "one heart and soul" (cf. *Ac* 4:32).

Mary as mother

Human life passes through various phases of transition, which are often difficult and demanding and which require binding choices, renunciation and sacrifice. The Mother of Jesus was placed by the Lord in the decisive moments of salvation history, and she always knew how to respond with complete availability - the fruit of a profound bond with God that had matured through assiduous and intense prayer. Between the Friday of the passion and the Sunday of the resurrection, the beloved disciple, and with him the entire community of disciples, was entrusted to her (cf. *Jn* 19:26). Between Ascension and Pentecost, she is found *with* and *in* the Church in prayer (cf. *Ac* 1:14). As Mother of God and Mother of the Church, Mary exercises her maternity until the end of history. Let us entrust every phase of our personal and ecclesial lives to her, not the least of which is our final passing. Mary teaches us the necessity of prayer, and she shows us that it is only through a constant, intimate, loving bond with her son that we may courageously leave "our home", ourselves, in order to reach the ends of the earth and everywhere announce the Lord Jesus, the Saviour of the world.

The Passover of the Lord

The certainty of Christ

After the solemn celebrations of Easter, our meeting today is imbued with spiritual joy. Although the sky is grey we carry in our hearts the joy of Easter, the certainty of the resurrection of Christ who triumphed over death once and for all. In the first place I renew to each one of you a cordial Easter greeting: may the joyful announcement of Christ's resurrection ring out in all homes and in all hearts so that hope may be reborn.

Fear and peace

In this Catechesis I would like to demonstrate the transformation that the Pasch of Jesus worked in his disciples. Let us start with the evening of the day of the resurrection. The disciples had locked the door to the house for fear of the Jews (cf. *Jn* 20:19). Fear caused their hearts to miss a beat, and prevented them from reaching out to others and to life. The Teacher was no longer. The memory of his passion gave rise to uncertainty. Yet Jesus had his followers at heart and was about to fulfil the promise he had made during the Last Supper: "I will not leave you desolate; I will come to you" (*Jn* 14:18) and he also says this to us, even in overcast weather: "I will not leave you desolate". With Jesus's arrival the disciple's situation of anguish changes radically. He enters through closed doors, he stands in their midst and gives them the peace that reassures: "Peace to you" (*Jn* 20:19b). It is a common greeting but it now acquires new significance because it brings about an inner change; it is the Easter greeting that enables the disciples to overcome all fear. The peace that Jesus brings is the gift of salvation that he had promised in his farewell discourses: "Peace I leave with you; my peace I give to you; not as the world gives do I give to you. Let not your hearts be troubled, neither let them be afraid" (*Jn* 14:27). On this day of the resurrection he gives it in fullness and for the community it becomes a source of joy, the certainty of victory, and security in relying on God. "Let not your hearts be troubled" (*Jn* 14:1), do not be afraid, he also says to us.

Sorrow becomes joy

After this greeting, Jesus shows the disciples the wounds in his hands and in his side (cf. *Jn* 20:20), signs of what has occurred and will never be cancelled: his glorious humanity remains "wounded". The purpose of this act is to confirm the new reality of the resurrection: Christ, now among his own, is a real person, the same Jesus who three days earlier was nailed to the cross. And it is in this way that in the dazzling light of Easter, in the encounter with the Risen One, the disciples perceive the salvific meaning of his passion and his death. Then sorrow and fear turn into full joy. The sorrow and the wounds themselves become a source of joy. The joy that is born in their hearts derives from "[having seen] the Lord" (*Jn* 20:20). He repeats to them: "Peace be with you" (v. 21). By then it was obvious that it was not only a greeting. It was a gift, *the* gift that the Risen One wants to offer his friends, but at the same time it is a consignment.

The disciples are sent out

This peace, which Christ purchased with his blood, is for them but also for all; the disciples must pass it on to the whole world. Indeed, he adds: "As the Father has sent me, even so I send you" (ibid). The Risen Jesus returned to his disciples to send them out. He had completed his work in the world, it was then up to them to sow faith in hearts so that the Father, known and loved, might gather all his children from the dispersion. But Jesus knows that his followers are still fearful, even now. Thus he carries out the gesture of blowing upon them and regenerates them in his Spirit (cf. *Jn* 20:22); this action is the sign of the new creation. In fact, with the gift of the Holy Spirit that comes from the Risen Christ, a new world begins. The sending of the disciples on mission is the beginning of the journey in the world of the people of the New Covenant, a people who believe in him and in his work of salvation, a people who witness to the truth of the resurrection. This newness of life that does not die, brought by Easter, must be spread everywhere so that the thorns of sin, which wound the human heart, leave room for the new shoots of Grace, of God's presence and of his love that triumph over sin and death.

Christ gives purpose

Today too the Risen One enters our homes and our hearts, even when, at times, the doors are closed. He enters giving joy and peace, life and hope, gifts we need for our human and spiritual rebirth. Only he can roll away those stones from the tombs in which all too often people seal themselves off from their own feelings, their own relationships, their own behaviour; stones that sanction death: division, enmity, resentment, envy, diffidence, indifference. Only he, the Living One, can give meaning to existence and enable those who are weary and sad, downhearted and drained of hope, to continue on their journey. This was the experience of the two disciples who were on their way from Jerusalem to Emmaus on Easter Day (cf. *Lk* 24:13-35). They were talking about Jesus but their sad looks (cf. v. 17), expressed their disappointed hopes, uncertainty and melancholy. They had left their homeland to follow Jesus with his friends and had discovered a new reality in which forgiveness and love were no longer only words but had a tangible effect on life. Jesus of Nazareth had made all things new, he had transformed their life. But now he was dead and it all seemed to be over.

The road to Emmaus

Suddenly, however, they are no longer two, but three people who are walking. Jesus joins the two disciples and walks with them, but they are unable to recognise him. They have of course heard the rumours about his resurrection, indeed they even tell him: "Some women of our company amazed us. They were at the tomb early in the morning and did not find his body; and they came back saying that they had even seen a vision of angels who said that he was alive" (vv. 22-23). Yet all this did not suffice to convince them, because "him they did not see" (v. 24). So Jesus, "beginning with Moses and all the prophets", patiently "interpreted to them in all the Scriptures the things concerning himself" (v. 27). The Risen One explains Sacred Scripture to the disciples, giving the fundamental key to reading it, namely, he himself and his Paschal Mystery: it is to him that the Scriptures bear witness (cf. *Jn* 5:39-47). The meaning of all things, of the Law, of the Prophets and of the Psalms, suddenly dawns on them and becomes clear to their eyes. Jesus had opened their minds to the understanding of the Scriptures (cf. *Lk* 24:45).

Word and Eucharist

In the meantime, they had reached the village, probably the home of one of the two. The unknown wayfarer "appeared to be going further" (v. 28), but then he stayed with them because they asked him to so insistently: "Stay with us" (v.

29). We too must say insistently to the Lord, over and over again, "Stay with us". "When he was at table with them, he took the bread and blessed and broke it, and gave it to them" (v. 30). The reference to Jesus's gestures at the Last Supper is evident. "And their eyes were opened and they recognised him" (v. 31). The presence of Jesus, first with words and then with the act of breaking the bread, enabled the disciples to recognise him and they could feel in a new way what they had felt while they were walking beside him: "Did not our hearts burn within us while he talked to us on the road, while he opened to us the Scriptures?" (v. 32). This episode points out to us two special "places" where we can encounter the Risen One who transforms our life: in listening to his word, in communion with Christ, and in the breaking of the bread; two "places" profoundly united with each other because "Word and Eucharist are so deeply bound together that we cannot understand one without the other: the word of God sacramentally takes flesh in the event of the Eucharist" (Post-Synodal Apostolic Exhortation, *Verbum Domini,* nn. 54-55).

The need to witness

After this encounter, the two disciples "rose that same hour and returned to Jerusalem; and they found the eleven gathered together and those who were with them, who said, 'The Lord has risen indeed, and has appeared to Simon!'" (v. 33-34). In Jerusalem they hear the news of

Jesus's resurrection and, in turn, they recount their own experience, on fire with love for the Risen One who has opened their hearts to an uncontainable joy. As St Peter says, they were "born anew to a living hope through the resurrection of Jesus Christ from the dead" (cf. *1 Pt* 1:3). Indeed, the enthusiasm of faith, love for the community and the need to communicate the Good News were reborn within them. The Teacher is risen and with him all life is reborn; witnessing to this event becomes an irrepressible need for them.

Our encounter with Christ

May the Easter season be for us all a favourable opportunity to rediscover the sources of faith, the presence of the Risen One among us, with joy and enthusiasm. It is a question of making the same journey that Jesus enabled the two disciples of Emmaus to make, by rediscovering the word of God and the Eucharist, that is, by walking with the Lord and letting our eyes be opened to the true meaning of Scripture and to his presence in the breaking of bread. The culmination of this journey, then as today, is Eucharistic Communion: in Communion Jesus nourishes us with his Body and his Blood, to be present in our life, to renew us, and to enliven us with the power of the Holy Spirit.

To conclude, the experience of the disciples invites us to think about the meaning of Easter for us. Let us allow ourselves to encounter the Risen Jesus! He, alive and true, is ever present in our midst; he walks with us to guide our life, to open our eyes. Let us trust in the Risen One who has the power to give life, to make us be born anew as children of God, capable of believing and of loving. Faith in him transforms our life: frees it from fear, gives it firm hope, enlivens it with God's love which gives full meaning to existence.

Little Pentecost

Presence of the Holy Spirit

After the great celebrations let us now return to the Catecheses on Prayer. At the Audience before Holy Week we reflected on the figure of the Blessed Virgin Mary and her prayerful presence among the Apostles while they were waiting for the descent of the Holy Spirit. The Church took her first steps in an atmosphere of prayer. Pentecost is not an isolated episode because the Holy Spirit's presence and action never cease to guide and encourage the Christian community as it journeys on. Indeed, in addition to recounting the event of the great outpouring in the Upper Room which occurred fifty days after Easter (cf. *Ac* 2:1-13), St Luke mentions in the *Acts of the Apostles* other extraordinary occasions on which the Holy Spirit burst in and which recur in the Church's history. And today I would like to reflect on what has been defined as the "little Pentecost", which took place at the height of a difficult phase in the life of the nascent Church.

Prayer in times of difficulty

The Acts of the Apostles tell that after the healing of a paralytic at the Temple of Jerusalem (cf. *Ac* 3:1-10), Peter and John were arrested (cf. *Ac* 4:1) for proclaiming Jesus's resurrection to all the people (cf. *Ac* 3:11-26). They were released after a hasty trial, joined their brethren and told them what they had been obliged to undergo on account of the witness they had born to Jesus, the Risen One. At that moment, Luke says, "they lifted their voices together to God" (*Ac* 4:24). Here St Luke records the Church's most extensive prayer in the New Testament, at the end of which, as we have heard, "the place in which they were gathered together was shaken; and they were all filled with the Holy Spirit and spoke the word of God with boldness" (*Ac* 4:31). Before reflecting on this beautiful prayer let us take note of an important basic attitude: when the first Christian community is confronted by dangers, difficulties and threats it does not attempt to work out how to react, find strategies, defend itself or what measures to adopt; rather, when it is put to the test, the community starts to pray and makes contact with God.

A community united in prayer

And what are the features of this prayer? It is a unanimous, concordant prayer of the entire community which reacts to persecution because of Jesus. In the original Greek, St Luke uses the word "*homothumadon*" - "all these with one accord", "in agreement", a term that appears in other parts of the *Acts of the Apostles* to emphasise this persevering, harmonious prayer (cf. *Ac* 1:14; 2:46). This harmony was the fundamental element of the first community and must always be fundamental to the Church. Thus it was not only the prayer prayed by Peter and John, who were in danger, but the prayer of the entire community since what the two Apostles were experiencing did not concern them alone but the whole of the Church. In facing the persecution it suffered for the cause of Jesus, not only was the community neither frightened nor divided but it was also deeply united in prayer, as one person, to invoke the Lord. I would say that this is the first miracle which is worked when, because of their faith, believers are put to the test. Their unity, rather than being jeopardised, is strengthened because it is sustained by steadfast prayer. The Church must not fear the persecutions which she has been subjected to throughout her history but must always trust, like Jesus at Gethsemane, in the presence, help and power of God, invoked in prayer.

The prayer asks for courage

Let us take a further step: what does the Christian community ask God at this moment of trial? It does not ask for the safety of life in the face of persecution, nor that the Lord get even with those who imprisoned Peter and John; it asks only that it be granted "to speak [his] word with all boldness" (*Ac* 4:29); in other words it prays that it may not lose the courage of faith, the courage to proclaim faith. First, however, it seeks to understand in depth what has occurred, to interpret events in the light of faith and it does so precisely through the word of God which enables us to decipher the reality of the world.

In the prayer it raises to the Lord the community begins by recording and invoking God's omnipotence and immensity: "Sovereign Lord, who did make the heaven and the earth and the sea and everything in them" (*Ac* 4:24). It is the invocation to the Creator: we know that all things come from him, that all things are in his hands. It is knowledge of this which gives us certainty and courage: everything comes from him, everything is in his hands. The prayer then goes on to recognise how God acted in the past - so it begins with the creation and continues through history - how he was close to his people, showing himself to be a God concerned with man, who did not withdraw, who did not abandon man, his creature; and here Psalm 2 is explicitly cited. It is in this light that the difficult situation the Church was going through at the time should be read.

Psalm 2

Psalm 2 celebrates the enthronement of the King of Judaea, but refers prophetically to the Coming of the Messiah, against whom human rebellion, persecution and abuse can do nothing: "Why do the nations conspire, and the people plot in vain? The kings of the earth set themselves, and the rulers take counsel together, against the Lord and against his Anointed?" (*Ps* 2:1-2; cf. *Ac* 4:25). The Psalm about the Messiah already stated this prophetically, and this uprising of the powerful against God's power is characteristic throughout history. It is precisely by reading Sacred

Scripture, which is the word of God, that the community can say to God in prayer: "Truly in this city there were gathered together against your holy servant Jesus, whom you did anoint, ...to do whatever your hand and your plan had predestined to take place" (*Ac* 4:27).

Interpretation

What happened is interpreted in the light of Christ, which is also the key to understanding persecution; and the cross, which is always the key to the resurrection. The opposition to Jesus, his passion and his death are reinterpreted through Psalm 2 as the actuation of God the Father's project for the world's salvation. And here we also find the meaning of the experience of persecution that the first Christian community was living through. This first community is not a mere association but a community that lives in Christ so what happens to it is part of God's plan. Just as it happened to Jesus, the disciples also meet with opposition, misunderstanding and persecution. In prayer, meditation on Sacred Scripture in the light of Christ's mystery helps us to interpret the reality present within the history of salvation which God works in the world, always in his own way.

Supplication

This is precisely why the request to God that the first Christian community of Jerusalem formulated in a prayer does not ask to be protected or to be spared trials and hardship. It is not a prayer for success but only to be able to proclaim the word of God with "*parresia*", that is, with boldness, freedom and courage (cf. *Ac* 4:29). Then there is the additional request that this proclamation may be guided by God's hand so that healing, signs and wonders may be performed, (cf. *Ac* 4:30), in other words that God's goodness may be visible as a power that transforms reality, that changes peoples' hearts, minds and lives and brings the radical newness of the Gospel.

The Holy Spirit

At the end of the prayer, St Luke notes, "the place in which they were gathered together was shaken; and they were all filled with the Holy Spirit and spoke the word of God with boldness" (*Ac* 4:31). The place shook, that is, faith has the power to transform the earth and the world. The same Spirit who spoke through Psalm 2 in the prayer of the Church bursts into the house and fills the hearts of all those who have invoked the Lord. This is the fruit of the unanimous prayer that the Christian community raises to God: the outpouring of the Spirit, a gift of the Risen One that sustains and guides the free and courageous proclamation of God's Word, which impels the disciples of the Lord to go out fearlessly to take the Good News to the ends of the world.

Victory of God

We too must be able to ponder the events of our daily life in prayer, in order to seek their deep meaning. And like the first Christian community let us too let ourselves be illuminated by the word of God, through meditation on Sacred Scripture, we can learn to see that God is present in our life, present also and especially in difficult moments and that all things - even those that are incomprehensible - are part of a superior plan of love in which the final victory over evil, over sin and over death is truly that of goodness, of grace, of life and of God.

Just as prayer helped the first Christian community, prayer also helps us to interpret our personal and collective history in the most just and faithful perspective, that of God. And let us too renew our request for the gift of the Holy Spirit, that warms hearts and enlightens minds, in order to recognise how the Lord hears our prayers, in accordance with his will of love and not with our own ideas. Guided by the Spirit of Jesus Christ, we will be able to live with serenity, courage and joy every situation in life and with St Paul boast: "We rejoice in our sufferings, knowing that suffering produces endurance, and endurance produces character, and character produces hope", hope that "does not disappoint us, because God's love has been poured into our hearts through the Holy Spirit who has been given to us" (*Rm* 5:3-5).

The Primacy of Prayer and of the Word of God

Problems in the Early Church

In our last Catechesis I explained that from the outset the Church has had to face unexpected situations on her journey, new issues and emergencies to which she has sought to respond in the light of faith, letting herself be guided by the Holy Spirit. Today I would like to pause to reflect on another of these situations, on a serious problem that the first Christian community of Jerusalem was obliged to face and to solve, as St Luke tells us in the sixth chapter of the *Acts of the Apostles*, concerning pastoral charity to lonely people and those in need of assistance and help. This is not a secondary matter for the Church and at that time risked creating divisions in the Church; the number of disciples, in fact continued to increase, but the Greek-speaking began to complain about those who spoke Hebrew because their widows were left out of the daily distribution (cf. *Ac* 6:1).

Discernment of the Apostles

To face this urgent matter which concerned a fundamental aspect of community life, namely, charity to the weak, the poor and the defenceless, and justice, the Apostles summoned the entire group of disciples. In that moment of pastoral emergency the Apostles' discernment stands out. They were facing the primary need to proclaim God's word in accordance with the Lord's mandate but - even if this was a priority of the Church - they considered with equal gravity the duty of charity and justice, that is, the duty to help widows and poor people and, in response to the commandment of Jesus: "love one another as I have loved you" (cf. *Jn* 15:12,17), to provide lovingly for their brothers and sisters in need. So it was that difficulties arose in the two activities that must coexist in the Church - the proclamation of the word, the primacy of God and concrete charity, justice - and it was necessary to find a solution so that there would be room for both, for their necessary relationship. The Apostles' reflection is very clear, they say, as we heard: "It is not right that we should give up preaching the word of God to serve tables. Therefore, brethren, pick out from among you seven men of good repute, full of the Spirit and of wisdom, whom we may appoint to this duty. But we will devote ourselves to prayer and to the ministry of the word" (*Ac* 6:2-4).

Social and spiritual actions

Two points stand out: first, since that moment a ministry of charity has existed in the Church. The Church must not only proclaim the word but must also put the word - which is charity and truth - into practice. And, the second point: these men must not only enjoy a good reputation but also they must be filled with the Holy Spirit and with wisdom; in other words they cannot merely be organisers who know what "to do", but must "act" in a spirit of faith with God's enlightenment, with wisdom of heart. Hence their role - although it is above all a practical one - has nonetheless also a spiritual function. Charity and justice are not only social but also spiritual actions, accomplished in the light of the Holy Spirit. We can thus say that the Apostles confronted this situation with great responsibility. They took the following decision: seven men were chosen; the Apostles prayed the Holy Spirit to grant them strength and then laid their hands on the seven so that they might dedicate themselves in a special way to this ministry of charity.

The example of Martha and Mary

Thus in the life of the Church, the first steps she took, in a certain way, reflected what had happened in Jesus's public life at Martha and Mary's house in Bethany. Martha was completely taken up with the service of hospitality to offer to Jesus and his disciples; Mary, on the contrary, devoted herself to listening to the Lord's word (cf. *Lk* 10:38-42). In neither case were the moments of prayer and of listening to God, and daily activity, the exercise of charity. Jesus's reminder, "Martha, Martha, you are anxious and troubled about many things; one thing is needful. Mary has chosen the good portion, which shall not be taken away from her" (*Lk* 10:41-42) and, likewise, the Apostles' reflection: "We will devote ourselves to prayer and to the ministry of the word" (*Ac* 6:4), show the priority we must give to God. I do not wish here to enter into the interpretation of this Martha-Mary passage. In any case activity undertaken to help one's neighbour, "the other", is not to be condemned, but it is essential to stress the need for it to be imbued also with the spirit of contemplation. Moreover, St Augustine says that this reality of Mary is a vision of our situation from heaven, so on earth we can never possess it completely but a little anticipation must be present in all our activities. Contemplation of God must also be present. We must not lose ourselves in pure activism but always let ourselves also be penetrated in our activities by the light of the word of God and thereby learn true charity, true service to others, which does not need many things - it certainly needs the necessary things - but needs above all our heartfelt affection and the light of God.

Comments from the Saints

In commenting on the episode of Martha and Mary St Ambrose urges his faithful and us too: "Let us too seek to have what cannot be taken from us, dedicating diligent, not distracted attention to the Lord's word. The seeds of the heavenly word are blown away if they are sown along the roadside. May the wish to know be an incentive to you too, as it was to Mary: this is the greatest and most perfect act". And he added that "attention to the ministry must not distract from knowledge of the heavenly word" through prayer (*Expositio Evangelii secundum Lucam,* VII, 85 *PL* 15, 1720). Saints have therefore experienced a profound unity of life between prayer and action, between total love for God and love for their brethren. St Bernard, who is a model of harmony between contemplation and hard work, in his book *De consideratione*, addressed to Pope Innocent II to offer him some reflections on his ministry, insists precisely on the importance of inner recollection, of prayer to defend oneself from the dangers of being hyper-active, whatever our condition and whatever the task to be carried out. St Bernard says that all too often too much work and a frenetic life-style end by hardening the heart and causing the spirit to suffer (cf.II, 3).

Daily prayer

His words are a precious reminder to us today, used as we are to evaluating everything with the criterion of productivity and efficiency. The passage from the *Acts of the Apostles* reminds us of the importance - without a doubt a true and proper ministry is created - of devotion to daily activities which should be carried out with responsibility and dedication and also our need for God, for his guidance, for his light which gives us strength and hope. Without daily prayer lived with fidelity, our acts are empty, they lose their profound soul, and are reduced to being mere activism which in the end leaves us dissatisfied. There is a beautiful invocation of the Christian tradition to be recited before any other activity which says: "*Actiones nostras, quæsumus, Domine, aspirando præveni et adiuvando prosequere, ut cuncta nostra oratio et operatio a te semper incipiat, et per te coepta finiatur*"; that is, "Inspire our actions, Lord, and accompany them with your help, so that our every word and action may always begin and end in you". Every step in our life, every action, of the Church too, must be taken before God, in the light of his word.

Prayer nourished by the word of God

In the last Catechesis the unanimous prayer of the first Christian community in times of trial was emphasised, and explained how, in prayer itself, in meditation on Sacred Scripture, the community was able to understand the events that were happening. When prayer is nourished by the word of God we can see reality with new eyes, with the eyes of faith and the Lord, who speaks to the mind and the heart, gives new light to the journey at every moment and in every situation. We believe in the power of the word of God and of prayer. Even the difficulties that the Church was encountering as she faced the problem of service to the poor, the issue of charity, was overcome in prayer, in the light of God, of the Holy Spirit. The Apostles did not limit themselves to ratifying the choice of Stephen and the other men but "they prayed and laid their hands upon them" (*Ac* 6:6). The Evangelist was once again to recall these gestures on the occasion of the election of Paul and Barnabas, where we read: "After fasting and praying they laid their hands on them and sent them off" (*Ac* 13:3). He confirms again that the practical service of charity is a spiritual service. Both these realities must go hand in hand.

Laying on of hands

With the act of the laying on of hands, the Apostles conferred a special ministry on seven men so that they might be granted the corresponding grace. The emphasis on prayer - "after praying", they say - is important because it highlights the gesture's spiritual dimension; it is not merely a question of conferring an office as happens in a public organisation, but is an ecclesial event in which the Holy Spirit appropriates seven men chosen by the Church, consecrating them in the Truth that is Jesus Christ: he is the silent protagonist, present during the imposition of hands so that the chosen ones may be transformed by his power and sanctified in order to face the practical challenges, the pastoral challenges. And the emphasis on prayer also reminds us that the response to the Lord's choice and the allocation of every ministry in the Church stems solely from a close relationship with God, nurtured daily.

The value of prayer

The pastoral problem that induced the Apostles to choose and to lay their hands on seven men charged with the service of charity, so that they themselves might be able to devote themselves to prayer and to preaching the word, also indicates to us the primacy of prayer and of the word of God which, however, then result in pastoral action. For pastors, this is the first and most valuable form of service for the flock entrusted to them. If the lungs of prayer and of the word of God do not nourish the breath of our spiritual life, we risk being overwhelmed by countless everyday things: prayer is the breath of the soul and of life. And there is another precious reminder that I would like to underscore: in the relationships with God, in listening to his word, in dialogue with God, even when we may be in the silence of a church or of our room, we are united in the Lord to a great many brothers and sisters in faith, like an ensemble of musical instruments which, in spite of their individuality, raise to God one great symphony of intercession, of thanksgiving and praise.

The Testimony of St Stephen

The prayer of the first Christian martyr

In our recent Catecheses we have seen how through personal and community prayer the interpretation of and meditation on Sacred Scripture open us to listening to God who speaks to us and instils light in us so that we may understand the present. Today, I would like to talk about the testimony and prayer of the Church's first martyr, St Stephen, one of the seven men chosen to carry out the service of charity for the needy. At the moment of his martyrdom, recounted in the Acts of the Apostles, the fruitful relationship between the word of God and prayer is once again demonstrated.

St Stephen before the council

Stephen is brought before the council, before the Sanhedrin, where he is accused of declaring that "this Jesus of Nazareth will destroy this place, [the Temple] and will change the customs which Moses delivered to us" (*Ac* 6:14). During his public life Jesus had effectively foretold the destruction of the Temple of Jerusalem: you will "destroy this temple, and in three days I will raise it up" (*Jn* 2:19). But, as the Evangelist John remarked, "he spoke of the temple of his body. When therefore he was raised from the dead, his disciples remembered that he had said this; and they believed the Scripture and the word which Jesus had spoken" (*Jn* 2:21-22).

Stephen's speech to the council, the longest in the *Acts of the Apostles*, develops on this very prophecy of Jesus who is the new Temple, inaugurates the new worship and, with his immolation on the cross, replaces the ancient sacrifices. Stephen wishes to demonstrate how unfounded is the accusation levelled against him of subverting the Mosaic law and describes his view of salvation history and of the covenant between God and man. In this way he reinterprets the whole of the biblical narrative, the itinerary contained in Sacred Scripture, in order to show that it leads to the "place" of the definitive presence of God that is Jesus Christ, and in particular his passion, death and resurrection. In this perspective Stephen also interprets his being a disciple of Jesus, following him even to martyrdom. Meditation on Sacred Scripture thus enables him to understand his mission, his life, his present. Stephen is guided in this by the light of the Holy Spirit and by his close relationship with the Lord, so that the members of the Sanhedrin saw that his face was "like the face of an angel" (*Ac* 6:15). This sign of divine assistance is reminiscent of Moses's face which shone after his encounter with God when he came down from Mount Sinai (cf. *Ex* 34:29-35; *2 Co* 3:7-8).

God's actions in the Old Testament

In his discourse Stephen starts with the call of Abraham, a pilgrim bound for the land pointed out to him by God which he possessed only at the level of a promise. He then speaks of Joseph, sold by his brothers but helped and liberated by God, and continues with Moses, who becomes an instrument of God in order to set his people free but also and several times comes up against his own people's rejection. In these events narrated in Sacred Scripture to which Stephen demonstrates he listens religiously, God always emerges, who never tires of reaching out to man in spite of frequently meeting with obstinate opposition. And this happens in the past, in the present and in the future. So it is that throughout the Old Testament he sees the prefiguration of the life of Jesus himself, the Son of God made flesh who - like the ancient Fathers - encounters obstacles, rejection and death. Stephen then refers to Joshua, David and Solomon, whom he mentions in relation to the building of the Temple of Jerusalem, and ends with the word of the Prophet Isaiah (66:1-2): "Heaven is my throne, and earth my footstool. What house will you build for me, says the Lord, or what is the place of my rest? Did not my hand make all these things?" (*Ac* 7:49-50).

God is present in Christ

In his meditation on God's action in salvation history, by highlighting the perennial temptation to reject God and his action, he affirms that Jesus is the Righteous One foretold by the prophets; God himself has made himself uniquely and definitively present in him: Jesus is the "place" of true worship. Stephen does not deny the importance of the Temple for a certain period, but stresses that "the Most High does not dwell in houses made with hands" (*Ac* 7:48). The new, true temple in which God dwells is his Son, who has taken human flesh; it is the humanity of Christ, the Risen One, who gathers the peoples together and unites them in the Sacrament of his Body and his Blood. The description of the temple as "not made by human hands" is also found in the theology of St Paul and in the Letter to the Hebrews; the Body of Jesus which he assumed in order to offer himself as a sacrificial victim for the expiation of sins, is the new temple of God, the place of the presence of the living God; in him, God and man, God and the world are truly in touch: Jesus takes upon himself all the sins of humanity in order to bring it into the love of God and to "consummate" it in this love. Drawing close to the cross, entering into communion with Christ, means entering this transformation. And this means coming into contact with God, entering the true temple.

St Stephen's hour of death

Stephen's life and words are suddenly cut short by the stoning, but his martyrdom itself is the fulfilment of his life and message: he becomes one with Christ. Thus his meditation on God's action in history, on the divine word which in Jesus found complete fulfilment, becomes participation in the very prayer on the cross. Indeed, before dying, Stephen cries out: "Lord Jesus, receive my spirit" (*Ac* 7:59), making his own the words of Psalm 31[30]:6 and repeating Jesus' last words on Calvary: "Father, into your hands I commit my spirit" (*Lk* 23:46). Lastly, like Jesus, he cries out with a loud voice facing those who were stoning him: "Lord, do not hold this sin against them" (*Ac* 7:60). Let us note that if on the one hand Stephen's prayer echoes Jesus', on the other it is addressed to someone else, for the entreaty is to the Lord himself, namely, to Jesus whom he contemplates in glory at the right hand of the Father: "Behold, I see the heavens opened, and the Son of man standing at the right hand of God" (v. 55).

Instructions for prayer

St Stephen's witness gives us several instructions for our prayers and for our lives. Let us ask ourselves: where did this first Christian martyr find the strength to face his persecutors and to go so far as to give himself? The answer is simple: from his relationship with God, from his communion with Christ, from meditation on the history of salvation, from perceiving God's action which reached its crowning point in Jesus Christ. Our prayers, too, must be nourished by listening to the word of God, in communion with Jesus and his Church.

A second element: St Stephen sees the figure and mission of Jesus foretold in the history of the loving relationship between God and man. He - the Son of God - is the temple that is not "made with hands" in which the presence of God the Father became so close as to enter our human flesh to bring us to God, to open the gates of heaven. Our prayer, therefore, must be the contemplation of Jesus at the right hand of God, of Jesus as the Lord of our, or my, daily life. In him, under the guidance of the Holy Spirit, we too can address God and be truly in touch with God, with the faith and abandonment of children who turn to a Father who loves them infinitely.

The Imprisonment and Release of St Peter

The Church prays for St Peter

Today I would like to touch upon the last episode in the life of St Peter recorded in the *Acts of the Apostles*, his imprisonment by order of Herod Agrippa, and his release through the marvellous intervention of the Angel of the Lord on the eve of his trial in Jerusalem (cf. *Ac* 12:1-17). The narrative is once again marked by the prayer of the Church. St Luke writes: "So Peter was kept in prison; but earnest prayer for him was made to God by the Church" (*Ac* 12:5). And, after having miraculously left the prison, on the occasion of his visit to Mary's house, the mother of John (also called Mark), it tells us "many were gathered together and were praying" (*Ac* 12:12). Between these two important observations that illustrate the attitude of the Christian community in the face of danger and persecution, is recounted the detainment and release of Peter, during the entire night. The strength of the unceasing prayer of the Church rises to God and the Lord listens and performs an unheard of and unexpected deliverance, sending his Angel.

Parallel events

The account reminds us of the great elements during Israel's deliverance from captivity in Egypt, the Hebrew

Passover. As happened in that major event, here also, the Angel of the Lord performs the primary action that frees Peter. And the actions of the Apostle - who is asked to rise quickly, put on his belt and gird his loins - repeat those of the Chosen People on the night of their deliverance through God's intervention, when they were invited to eat the lamb quickly with their belts fastened, sandals on their feet, and their staffs in their hands, ready to leave the country (cf. *Ex* 12:11). Thus, Peter could exclaim: "Now I am sure that the Lord has sent his Angel and rescued me from the hand of Herod" (*Ac* 12:11). The Angel does not only recall the deliverance of Israel from Egypt, but also the resurrection of Christ. Recounted in the *Acts of the Apostles*: "And behold, an Angel of the Lord appeared, and a light shone in the cell; and he struck Peter on the side and woke him" (*Ac* 12:7). The light that fills the prison cell, the same action to awaken the Apostle, refers to the liberating light of the Passover of the Lord that triumphs over the darkness of night and evil. Finally, the invitation to "Wrap your mantle around you and follow me" (*Ac* 12:8) echoes the words of the initial call of Jesus in our hearts (cf. *Mk* 1:17), repeated after the resurrection on Lake Tiberias, where on two occasions the Lord says to Peter, "Follow me" (*Jn* 21:19, 22). It is a pressing call to follow him. Only by coming out of ourselves to walk with the Lord and by doing his will can we live in true freedom.

The faith of St Peter

I would also like to highlight another aspect of Peter's attitude in prison. In fact, we note that while the Christian community is praying earnestly for him, Peter "was sleeping" (*Ac* 12:6). In a critical situation of serious danger, it is an attitude that might seem strange, but instead denotes tranquillity and faith. He trusts God. He knows he is surrounded by the solidarity and prayers of his own people and completely abandons himself into the hands of the Lord. So it must be with our prayer, assiduous, in solidarity with others, fully trusting that God knows us in our depths and takes care of us to the point that Jesus says "even the hairs of your head are all numbered. Fear not, therefore" (*Mt* 10:30-31). Peter lives through that night of imprisonment and release from prison as a moment of his discipleship with the Lord who overcomes the darkness of night and frees him from the chains of slavery and the threat of death. His is a miraculous release, marked by various accurately described steps, guided by the Angel, despite the monitoring of the guards, through the first and second guard posts, up to the iron doors to exit to the city, with the door opening by itself in front of them (cf. *Ac* 12:10). Peter and the Angel of the Lord make their way together down a stretch of the street until, coming back to himself, the Apostle realises that the Lord really freed him and, after having reflected on the matter, goes to the house of Mary the mother of Mark where many disciples were gathered in prayer. Once again the community's response to difficulty and danger is to trust in God, strengthening the relationship with him.

Praying wrongly and well

Here it seems useful to recall another difficult situation that the early Christian community experienced. St James speaks of it in his Letter. It is a community in crisis, in difficulty, not so much because of persecution, but because of the jealousies and contentions within it (cf. *Jm* 3:14-16). The Apostle wonders about the reason for this situation. He finds two primary motives. The first is that they let themselves be carried away by their emotions, by the dictates of their own interests, by selfishness (cf. *Jm* 4:1-2a). The second is the lack of prayer - "you do not ask" (*Jm* 4:2b) - or a kind of a prayer that cannot qualify as such - "You ask and do not receive, because you ask wrongly, to spend it on your passions" (*Jm* 4:3). This situation would change, according to St James, if the community all spoke together with God, truly praying assiduously and unanimously. In fact, even talking about God runs the risk of losing inner strength and the testimony dries up if they are not animated, sustained and accompanied by prayer, by continuity of a living dialogue with the Lord. An important reminder also for us and our communities, both the small ones like the family and the bigger ones like the parish, the diocese and the entire Church. And it makes me think that they prayed in this community of St James, but prayed wrongly, solely for their own passions. We must always learn again how to pray properly, truly pray, moving towards God and not towards our own good.

Unison with the Church and with Christ

Instead, the community that is concerned about Peter's imprisonment is a community that truly prays the entire night, deeply united. And it is overwhelming joy that fills the hearts of all when the Apostle unexpectedly knocks at the door. It is joy and amazement in light of the actions of the God who listens. Thus, from the Church arises the prayer for Peter and to the Church he returns to tell "how the Lord had brought him out of the prison" (*Ac* 12:17). In that Church where he is set as a rock (cf. *Mt* 16:18), Peter recounts his "Passover" of liberation. He experiences true freedom in following Jesus. He is enveloped in the radiant light of the resurrection and can therefore testify to the point of martyrdom that the Lord is risen and "sent his Angel and rescued me from the hand of Herod" (*Ac* 12:11). The martyrdom he was to suffer in Rome later will definitively unite him with Christ, who had told him: "When you are old, another will take you where you do not want to go, to show by what kind of death he was to glorify God" (cf. *Jn* 21:18-19).

Power through prayer

The episode of the liberation of Peter as told by Luke tells us that the Church, each of us, goes through the night of trial. But it is unceasing vigilance in prayer that sustains us. I too, from the first moment of my election as the Successor of St Peter, have always felt supported by your prayer, by the prayers of the Church, especially in moments of great difficulty. My heartfelt thanks. With constant and faithful prayer the Lord releases us from the chains, guides us through every night of imprisonment that can gnaw at our hearts. He gives us the peace of heart to face the difficulties of life, persecution, opposition and even rejection. Peter's experience shows us the power of prayer. And the Apostle, though in chains, feels calm in the certainty of never being alone. The community is praying for him. The Lord is near him. He indeed knows that Christ's "power is made perfect in weakness" (*2 Co* 12:9). Constant and unanimous prayer is also a precious tool to overcome any trial that may arise on life's journey, because it is being deeply united to God that allows us also to be united to others.

Sources

This book draws together the Wednesday Audience Catecheses of Pope Benedict XVI, which took place between the 14 March 2011 - 9 May 2012. This Catechesis series continues in the CTS publication *Prayer in the Letters of St Paul*.

The Prayerful Presence of the Blessed Virgin: General Audience, 14 March 2011, Saint Peter's Square.

The Passover of the Lord: General Audience, 11 April 2012, Saint Peter's Square.

Little Pentecost: General Audience, 18 April 2012, Saint Peter's Square.

The primacy of prayer and of the Word: General Audience, 25 April 2012, Saint Peter's Square.

The Testimony of St Stephen: General Audience, 2 May 2012, Saint Peter's Square.

The Imprisonment and Release of St Peter: General Audience, 9 May 2012, Saint Peter's Square.

The Acts of the Apostles

"Holiness and prayer is inconceivable without a renewed listening to the word of God - a life-giving encounter, which directs and shapes our lives."

- John Paul II

The Acts of the Apostles was penned by the same author as the Gospel of Luke. It is a gripping story which follows the adventures of Paul and the other Apostles taking the gospel to the ends of the earth. Contains the famous Pentecost narrative and the vital role of the Holy Spirit in the newly formed Church.

The Acts is introduced by Henry Wansbrough OSB who also gives practical guidance for personal reading and reflection. The Jerusalem Bible translation is that read in Church. The four gospels and the psalms are also available from CTS in the same format.

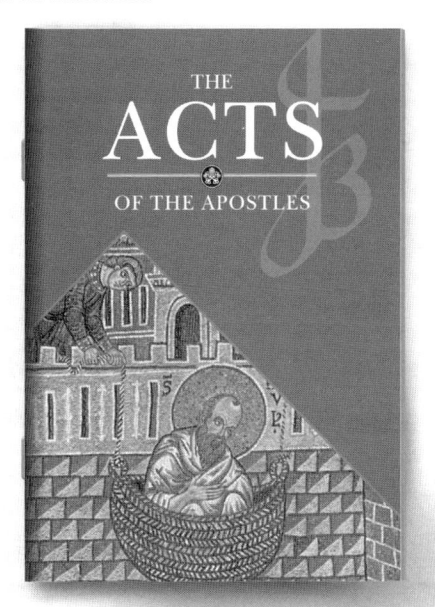

A world of Catholic reading at your fingertips...

Catholic Faith, Life & Truth for all

CTS
www.CTSbooks.org

twitter: @CTSpublishers

facebook.com/CTSpublishers

Catholic Truth Society, Publishers to the Holy See.